PERO

PERO

The Life of a Slave in Eighteenth-Century Bristol

Christine Eickelmann
David Small

Redcliffe Press in association with
Bristol Museums & Art Gallery

First published by Redcliffe Press Ltd, 81g Pembroke Road, Bristol BS8 3EA,
in association with Bristol Museums & Art Gallery, in 2004

ISBN 1 904537 03 0

British Library Cataloguing-in-Publication Data
A catalogue record for this book is available from the British Library.

Design and typesetting by Stephen Morris Communications, smc@freeuk.com, Bristol and Liverpool, and printed by HSW Print, Tonypandy, Rhondda.

CONTENTS

ACKNOWLEDGEMENTS

Our grateful thanks are due to Michael Richardson and Hannah Lowery at Bristol University Library's Department of Special Collections for their many kindnesses during the research for this book, and to the staffs at the archives of the Bristol Record Office, the Nevis Historical and Conservation Society and the Nevis Court House, Charlestown. We are most grateful to the Pinney family for permission to quote from the Pinney Papers and to John and Barbara Tobin for their help and interest.

Many people on Nevis have helped and sustained us during our visits to the island, and afterwards, as friends, have patiently dealt with our seemingly endless questions. In particular we would like to say thanks to Suzanne Gordon, Anne Hersh, Vince Hubbard, David and Joan Robinson and David and Nancy Rollinson.

We would especially like to thank Stephen Price, Director of Bristol Museums & Art Gallery, for suggesting the initial research and for his continuing help. The staff at Bristol Museums & Art Gallery have been most helpful with illustrations and we have very much appreciated the assistance given by Sue Giles in particular, but also by Jeremy Dixon, Alan Justin and Sheena Stoddard. We are also grateful to Madge Dresser of the University of the West of England and Peter Courtier and Eric Jay of the Bristol Racial Equality Council for their comments and suggestions.

Picture Acknowledgements

All pictures courtesy of Bristol Museums & Art Gallery except the following:

Front cover and page 8	Courtesy of Bristol United Press
Back cover and 23	Courtesy of the British Library (1786.c.9 Pl IV)
page: 21,24	Courtesy of University of Bristol Library, Special Collections
25, 56	Courtesy of J S Udal
26	Courtesy of St Christopher Heritage Society
27	Courtesy of Tim Taylor, Time Team
31, 42	Courtesy of Private Collection
48	Courtesy of Private Collection
59	Courtesy of Stephen Morris

13, 15, 20, 22, 29, 30, 37, 45, 46 and 52 the authors

FOREWORD

Our knowledge of the experience of enslaved Africans and black servants relies largely on just a handful of first-hand accounts, of which that by Olauda Equiano is the best known. These autobiographies, with their harrowing descriptions of conditions on board the ships which transferred Africans from their homeland and their treatment on the Caribbean sugar plantations, are principal sources for understanding the experience of the millions who were sold into slavery.

For most slaves though the source material is very thin, and although sometimes we learn their names and can track their sale into slavery, they remain part of a largely undocumented human cargo. It is therefore fascinating to follow the experiences of one slave-servant, Pero Jones, who was born in the Caribbean, sold as a child and worked for a Bristol sugar plantation owner for over thirty years. From the Caribbean island of Nevis Pero moved with his master, John Pinney, to Bristol where he assumed domestic duties as his principal male servant in Pinney's newly built house (now the Georgian House Museum).

Christine Eickelmann and David Small have meticulously pieced together Pero's life from a wide range of documentary sources. Their research began in the late 1990s to inform a display at the Georgian House, generating considerable interest in Pero's life. This has enabled us to stage living history events, drawing new audiences to the museum. More visibly, this focus on a Bristol slave led to the naming of the new bridge in Harbourside as Pero's Bridge in 1999.

This book not only presents the evidence for Pero's life as a slave-servant, but sets his experiences in a wider context of Bristol's role in the eighteenth-century transatlantic slave trade. We owe a great deal to the authors in telling a story that gives us a remarkable insight into this hidden history.

Stephen Price
Head of Museums & Art Gallery
Bristol

PERO JONES

Pero was an enslaved man, born in the West Indies, owned by the sugar planter and merchant John Pinney whose Bristol home is now the Georgian House Museum in Great George Street. Pero lived in that house for a number of years and, since a footbridge in Harbourside was named after him in March 1999, his name has become a familiar one in the city.

The bridge commemorates, and pays tribute to, all those Africans and West Indians who were enslaved by Bristol's merchants and planters. Pero is a symbol of the millions of men, women and children taken from their homes in Africa to the Americas as the central commodity in the transatlantic slave trade. Their toil in the North American and Caribbean plantations made people like Pinney rich, and by the time Pero came to Bristol in the 1780s, the city had become wealthy on the proceeds of the slave trade and plantation slavery.

BRISTOL'S PROSPERITY

About thirty years after Pero's death, the pro-slavery Member of Parliament James Evan Baillie acknowledged the source of much of Bristol's wealth in a placard he used in his 1830 election campaign but neglected to mention the debt the city owed to her trade with Africa:

> Bristol owes ALL her prosperity, nay, ... her existence to her commerce with the WEST INDIES. Without it she must sink to rise no more. Picture ... her now crowded streets, grass-grown and desolate – her glittering shops deserted, and the doors shut in her Streets!!! [1]

One of John Pinney's sons, Charles, applauded Baillie's subsequent election win: 'I am quite delighted we were so successful against our anti-slavery opponents in the Bristol election; they will be hardly daring enough to show their heads a second time.' Charles Pinney was wrong; only a few years later the system of slavery was abolished in the British colonies.

The Baillies, related to the Pinneys by marriage, had made a considerable fortune from slaves, sugar, and shipping, and although by the time Baillie wrote his election manifesto Britain had long ceased trading in slaves, freedom for existing slaves was still to come. Earlier, during Pero's lifetime, when 'the Demagogues for Abolition' thought of 'the most effective way to destroy the Slave Trade', John Pinney had expressed his dismay at the very idea that the seemingly never-ending supply of African slaves might cease. He warned of the 'deep stab to West India Credit and the value of Property', and the 'fatal consequences to some of our Islands'. This crisis he alluded to was caused by social and political pressures in Britain and by slave rebellions taking place all over the Caribbean, and, according to Pinney, 'Gentlemen who possess West India property were never in so critical a situation, they are truly to be pitied'. Their valuable West India properties were, of course, not just the plantations but also the enslaved people who laboured on them.

The Transatlantic Slave Trade

ENGLAND ENTERED the large-scale, systematic transatlantic slave trade soon after settlers established their North American and Caribbean tobacco and sugar plantations in the first half of the seventeenth century although, from as early as the mid-fifteenth century, other European nations had traded in African slaves.

Initially, settlers had used native Indian peoples but these died out rapidly from overwork, disease and maltreatment. Planters soon deemed Africans as most suitable for work in tropical conditions when white 'indentured labourers'[2] alone were not sufficient to fulfil their demand for a cheap and durable labour force. In the plantations enslaved Africans grew sugar, coffee, cotton, rice and tobacco. The colonial produce was then shipped to Britain and some re-exported to Europe.

This moving of goods, people and produce is often called the Triangular Trade but in practice the routes were more complex: many ships made return journeys from Europe directly to the Caribbean, there was trade between the Caribbean islands and North America, and some direct traffic between America, the Caribbean and Africa.

Africans, of course, did not go into slavery willingly. At every step along the way there was resistance: reports spoke of revolts in the holding forts, of men freeing slaves from ships lying in harbour, and of uprisings on board ship. Once on the plantations, the struggle for dignity and freedom continued in many different ways, either individually or collectively. Enslaved people damaged or stole animals, tools and crops, misunderstood orders, avoided work, or simply escaped. But there were also those who found they could gain advantages by outwardly complying with slavery, while at the same time fighting it, as did some of those women who willingly became planters' mistresses. According to one historian, 'the slaves who appeared to be well-assimilated into the world of their masters – domestics and skilled artisans – were in effect the most adept at this resistance within accommodation'.[3]

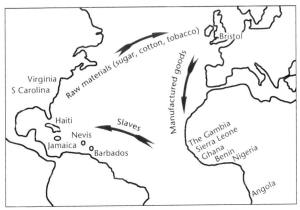

The 'triangle' of the Transatlantic slave trade

A View of ye Jason Privateer
Nicholas Pocock,
c.1760
Bristol privateers like
the *Jason* also acted as
slavers.

Estimates vary but generally it is reckoned that Portuguese, Spanish, English, French, Dutch and Danish vessels shipped between 11 and 13 million Africans across the Atlantic. Bristol's official participation in the Africa, or Guinea, trade – as it was politely called – only started when the monopoly of the London-controlled Royal Africa Company ended in 1698 but Bristol ships probably were involved in trading slaves illegally long before then. Bristol, well established as England's second port after London, had traded for centuries with Ireland and mainland Europe and was thus well positioned to take its lucrative slice of the Africa trade: it had the infrastructure – the port, the ships, the warehouses – and people with the know-how of international commerce. By around 1730 the city became the major slaving port, with about 50 voyages a year, accounting for almost half of all the ships leaving for Africa from the three major English slaving ports. Bristol ships varied in size from 30 to 420 tons, carrying up to 600 slaves from Africa on a single voyage.

Having eclipsed London, Bristol lost its leading position to Liverpool during the mid-1740s. By 1807, when Britain ended its part in the slave trade, Bristol ships had made over 2,000 slaving voyages and had carried about half a million people, perhaps a fifth of the British total.[4]

Trading goods for people

IN AFRICA, SLAVES were traded for goods shipped from Europe. Thus, on 5 March 1759 the Bristol owners of the snow *Swift* ordered James McTaggart to 'barter the whole of our cargo for as many fine young and healthy full grown negroes', as well as ivory. Goods sent from Bristol included cloth, guns and gunpowder, alcohol, iron bars and copper articles. A number of these were manufactured locally but many were imported from, for instance, Germany (linen) or Sweden (iron bars). Some items were mere trinkets but Africans also demanded quality merchandise. They were astute businessmen: not only did they have long-standing trading links with North Africa and the Middle East, they also had long experience of selling human beings.[5]

Some of the African masters sold their slaves to the Europeans, and James Fraser, commander of several ships from Bristol, hence claimed that 'most of the slaves we purchase at Bonny confess themselves to have [already] been slaves'.[6] However, it is generally accepted now that at least half of the enslaved people taken to the Americas were war captives, fewer than a third were those accused, or convicted, of crime or adultery, and perhaps one sixth were abducted. Africans usually did the kidnapping; Europeans wanted to be on good terms with locals and were generally not allowed to penetrate the interior.

Countless people perished on the arduous trek to the coast and while being imprisoned

Fort St George, Elmina, in present-day Ghana
Built by the Portuguese in the 1480s at a place they named El Mina, 'the mine', believing that the area was rich in gold. In 1637 Elmina, from which the term 'Mina negroe' was derived, became the Dutch slaving headquarters and subsequently passed to the British.

in the holding forts that lined the shores of Sierra Leone, Ghana and Nigeria. In dark, humid, stinking cells they spent their last few weeks or months on African soil. At some stage they were branded with 'burning irons' embossed with the name of the various companies, to avoid confusing slaves owned by different traders.

Most of the Bristol ships sailed to the coast of West Africa but some operated as far as Angola and even Mozambique. A normal round trip took about 12 to 15 months but could last much longer. Conditions for sailors on board ship were hard and dangerous, not just while waiting for their human cargo off the African coast. Usually ships were ready to sail within about four months but in some cases they waited up to seven or eight months.

The Middle Passage

ON BOARD SHIP, people usually lay shackled and cramped together on shelves, with perhaps a metre of space between layers. Twice daily the captives were fed a mash of boiled horse beans, rice, corn or yam, sometimes flavoured with a bit of meat or fish. People were seasick, homesick, hungry and thirsty. They developed sores and diseases. The freed slave Olaudah Equiano wrote about his terrible 'Middle Passage':

The closeness of the place, and the heat of the climate, added to the number in the ship, which was so crowded that each had scarcely room to turn himself, almost suffocated us. … The shrieks of the women, and the groans of the dying, rendered the whole a scene of horror almost inconceivable.[7]

The passage across the Atlantic usually lasted from six to 12 weeks. It has been estimated that about one African in eight died although mortality varied greatly with time, weather conditions, the length of the voyage, and the age and condition of the slaves. However, losses such as on the Bristol slaver *Mary* were not uncommon: on her voyage from Nigeria to Jamaica about half of the 300 slaves perished, as well as 20 from a crew of 36.

Once in a Caribbean port, sailors cleaned their ships and the slaves. Sales, advertised beforehand, either took place on board ship, or in slave markets. They were a big social occasion, and a planter from St Croix wrote that 'All the citizens of the island are present at such a sale and it is a pleasant thing to watch, as all those people sit, stand or lie down roundabout the auction site'.[8] Ahead lay, as one West Country planter put it, a life of 'extreme drudgery'. Enslaved people were property that could be sold, mortgaged, willed, or simply given away as gifts. Only a lucky few could hope to be freed by their owner, or to purchase their own freedom.

Slave Market, Charlestown, Nevis
It is unclear whether it was where slaves were sold or where they held their Sunday Market.

FOR THEIR RETURN journeys the slaving ships were re-fitted, so that they could carry the bulky hogsheads (large wooden barrels) full of sugar, rum or molasses. By the time ships were back in Bristol, after five to seven weeks, some of the enslaved people they had carried were dead already on the plantations but merchants and investors now counted their profits. These ranged from about 10 per cent for an average voyage to as much as 100 per cent, on an outlay of perhaps £4,000-8,000. However, if too many slaves had died, or the ship had been wrecked, gains quickly turned to losses.

By 1807, when Britain's involvement in the slave trade ceased, Bristol's share had slumped to a fraction. All over the Caribbean slaves were in open rebellion, demanding freedom from slavery, and while there was a strong movement by abolitionists and politicians in Britain to end the Africa trade, unsurprisingly many people tried to resist all pressures. Bristolians had a vested interest in prolonging the slave trade and, more importantly, plantation slavery. A large number of people benefited from either, or both, directly or indirectly. Not only did they build the ships, finance the voyages and manufacture the

Prince Street, Bristol in 1825, Edward Cashin, 1825
As merchants the Pinneys warehoused sugars in Prince Street and Farr's Lane at least until 1819.

goods for Africa, they also supplied the plantations with all the necessaries, went to the Americas to work as managers, overseers, and craftsmen, and processed the colonial produce in their Bristol sugar refineries and tobacco factories. Anchor smiths, butchers, brick-makers, and coopers – almost everybody in the city had a stake in the slave trade, or in slavery. But the tentacles of slavery spread well beyond the city into the West Country: in Somerset, for instance, J & M Mitchell, a clothier from Watchet, supplied 'negroe clothing', and sails made by John Bullock in East Coker were exported to the West Indies.

After the trade in slaves was abolished, it is again not surprising – given the economic benefits – that many people resisted moves to end slavery in the British colonies. However, a sweetener of £20 million paid by the British government in 1834 to slave owners made 'matters agreeable to the West Indians' – to the merchants and planters but not to the slaves. They got nothing, not even their freedom, for on most British islands they had to undergo a period of 'apprenticeship' during which they only received wages for part of their work. Complete emancipation did not come until August 1838, almost exactly forty years after Pero's death.

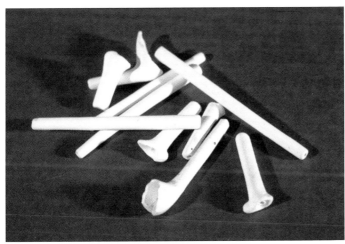

Clay pipe stems found in the waters off Pinney's Beach, Nevis
Many small Bristol workshops manufactured tobacco clay pipes which were exported to Africa and the Americas.

Slave-servants in Britain

PERO WAS ONE OF THOUSANDS of slave-servants who lived in Britain from the seventeenth century until the abolition of slavery. As a 'by-product' of the slave trade, a few came directly from Africa via the West Indies as part-payment to ships captains, so-called 'privilege' slaves, but most arrived from the West Indies. The majority were young males who came with their masters: plantation owners like Pinney, or merchants, soldiers and colonial administrators. In the West Indies they may have belonged to a large contingent of domestic servants of perhaps as many as 20 or 30, but usually they were brought to Britain singly, or in small groups. In addition to these slave-servants there were also free black people who earned a living as craftsmen, traders, labourers, musicians, or as scholars, soldiers, and sailors. Indeed, there was a black presence all over Europe, including countries that did not trade in slaves such as Russia and Germany.

Slave-servants were not paid wages. Thus they were cheaper than local labour but, as has been pointed out by historians of the black community in England, black servants performed another important function: they 'conferred on their masters and mistresses "an air of luxurious well being". They were at once charming, exotic ornaments, objects of curiosity, talking points and, above all, symbols of prestige'[9] and were treated accordingly: not cruelly but with a great deal of condescension. They adorned the households of aristocratic and well-to-do families, and many paintings of the period captured their role as 'luxury items'. The painter and engraver William Hogarth, on the other hand, portrayed some of those black people who were operating on the margins of society. In the tavern scene in his series *A Rake's Progress*, for instance, he depicts a black woman in the company of whores and drunks. Standing at the back of the group, she may have been a maid in the tavern, or she may have run away from domestic service. Many women were forced into prostitution to avoid starving to death. The story of Mary Prince illustrates the dilemma: born in Bermuda, she was sold to Antigua from where she came to England in about 1828. Whilst in London, she wanted to run away 'but I was a stranger, and did not know one door in the street from another, and was unwilling to go away'.[10] Her life was one of hardship and abuse, and as a female domestic she faced the additional burden of sexual exploitation but she strove to maintain her dignity. As the preface to her memoirs states, 'She demonstrates how a woman can be enslaved and yet not be a slave'.[11]

Mary Prince told her own life story and, as there are very few accounts of black female servants, her memoirs are all the more important as a historical source. A few of the lives of male slave-born servants have been well chronicled, particularly if they had a high public profile, either through their association with the rich and famous of the day, or through their own writings. Among them was Francis Barber, a man from Jamaica who worked for the writer Samuel Johnson, and to whom Johnson bequeathed valuable property and an annuity. Associated with Johnson was another well-known slave-born manservant, Ignatius Sancho. Thomas Gainsborough painted his portrait, and he was a friend of the great actor of the day, David Garrick. Sancho became a familiar figure in literary London, and his letters were published two years after his death in 1780. Two slave-born Africans, (Quobna) Ottobah Cugoano and Olaudah Equiano, also wrote their own life stories, as well as widely circulated anti-slavery books and articles. Cugoano, who only briefly was a manservant, came to England with his master from Grenada in the early 1770s, was set free, and by the mid-1780s had become a well-known member of the anti-slavery movement. The Nigerian-born Equiano arrived with a ship's captain via Barbados and Virginia. He was a servant, sailor, slave-driver turned anti-slavery campaigner and has been described as the 'first political leader of Britain's black community'.[12]

Pero was not famous in his lifetime and his personal achievements may not have been particularly outstanding, but he, too, deserves his place in history. He is one of the few anonymous slave-born servants whose life story is now known, but, as there were no records left by him, his life has had to be pieced together from the little John Pinney wrote about him in account books and letters. Of course he did not exist in isolation but had a family, was a member of the black communities in Nevis and Bristol and was a servant in the Pinney household. With this in mind, it is important to relate Pero both to the people around him and to the period in which he lived. Any account of his life, however, can be only an interpretation of the available evidence. No one will truly know how he felt about life as a slave-servant.

Pero's early years with John Pinney

IN HIS EARLY TWENTIES John Pinney (1740-1818) inherited from his Dorset cousin, John Frederick Pinney, property in the West Country and sugar plantations on the island of Nevis, one of the Leeward Islands in the West Indies. At Christmas 1764 John Pinney landed on Nevis to supervise the running of his plantations, one of which was called Mountravers.

He found the plantations run down. Many of the 140 slaves were too old, sick or disabled to work. He freed those he considered a burden on the estate, whilst continuing their allowances of food and clothes, and began replacing them. Pero, with his sisters Nancy and Sheeba and a 25-year-old enslaved African woman, Harriott, belonged to the second group of slaves Pinney bought, on 4 July 1765, from a Joanna Jones. The four cost £115 sterling/£195 Nevis currency (N£).[13] Extensive research in the Nevis Court House has revealed the original bill of sale documenting this transaction.

Pero was said to be twelve, Nancy eight and Sheeba six years old. Described as Creoles (that is, island-born), they were probably

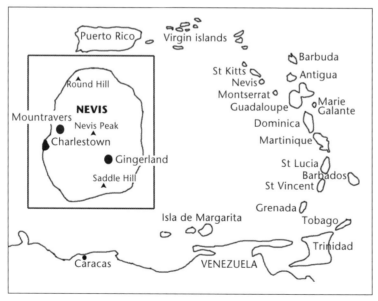

Map of the Caribbean showing Nevis and Pinney's Mountravers and Gingerland estates

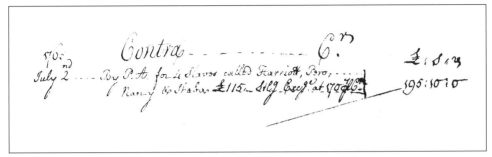

Entry in a Pinney ledgerbook recording the purchase of Pero, July 1765

born on Nevis. Pero's father may have been called William, and it is likely that he, too, was one of Joanna Jones's slaves. All we know of the children's family is that both parents were black and that Pero's father and another sister of his, Eve, were alive in 1798.

Pero is not an uncommon name among enslaved men on Nevis. It is possible that the name came from the Yoruba people in modern Nigeria where 'Pere' means 'made to open wide', or from the Bambara in the Upper Niger Valley where it means 'a noise, to cry loud'. However, alternatively, it may be a version of Portuguese, Spanish or French names, such as Pirro or Perreau. Pinney certainly used the latter spelling on a couple of occasions.

Nevis, a small island with strong Bristol and West Country connections, measures about eight miles by six. Around the time of Pero's

birth, its population was estimated at about 8,400 black and 1,000 white people. Enslaved people were regularly bought and sold, and it is likely that a fellow-planter recommended these four as a good investment to the newly arrived Englishman. Against the odds the children had survived the early childhood years and were old enough to be put to work. Born into slavery, they were adapted to life on the island. Harriott, on the other hand, was a 'seasoned' African woman. She had undergone the usual 'seasoning' period of three to five years in which enslaved Africans were forced to adjust to the hardships of plantation work in the West Indies.

Soon after being bought, Pero became Pinney's personal servant; he may have been earmarked by his previous owner for domestic work. At first Pero, Nancy, Sheeba and Harriott may have worked on Pinney's

Gingerland plantation but during 1767 certainly were on Pinney's main estate, Mountravers, in the parish of St Thomas Lowland, on the other side of the island. Sixty-five slaves remained on Gingerland. New purchases were distributed between the two plantations until, in September 1768, Pinney rented out Gingerland, removed all his slaves and concentrated his activities on Mountravers. Each time

Nevis from the sea
From 1780 Mountravers plantation (centre) ran from the sea to the top of the mountain.

people were moved, they had to settle into new housing, possibly adapt to different working methods and re-form relationships with fellow slaves, overseers and managers.

Mountravers plantation

DURING PERO'S TIME, Mountravers was a sugar plantation of 273 acres, stretching from the sea halfway up the island's mountain. Pinney's wooden house was in a 'cool and pleasant' situation, about two miles from the capital Charlestown. On the plantation were cattle mills, boiling and distilling houses, stables for mules and camels, and work-shops for carpenters and coopers. The main business of the plantation was to produce sugar, which involved several laborious processes: slaves planted the sugar cane in carefully dug holes in fields, and manured and weeded these. After about 15 months, they cut the mature stalks, bundled them together and, in the sugar factory, fed the

Slaves Cutting Sugar Cane from ***Ten Views in the Island of Antigua***, William Clark, 1823

Mountravers slave list, 1769
This list shows those people who were bought from 1764 onwards and had survived until 1 January 1769.

stems through mill rollers to extract the juice. This they then boiled in a succession of kettles, or coppers, until the head boiler judged the thick and very hot syrup ready for transferring into lined wooden trays. As the syrup cooled, sugar crystals formed. The brown mass, now called muscovado sugar, was transferred into large wooden casks, or hogsheads, for the molasses to drain out. The molasses was either consumed, exported, or distilled into rum. Once the sugar had 'cured' sufficiently, the hogsheads were ready for loading onto ships that took the sugar to England for refining.

All the work had to be done speedily, otherwise the cane juice went sour, or the sugar set to a mass of brown concrete. Making sugar was hard, physical labour, in a demanding climate. On Mountravers, between 1765 and mid-1770 more than forty men, women and children, out of a total of about 250, died from old age, accidents, sickness, or by committing suicide and, no doubt, in those early years of Pinney's management, overwork. He replenished his 'stock' of slaves with about 100 new purchases but sold some again, particularly those who persistently tried to escape.

The majority of slaves bought were Africans although Pinney later wrote that he preferred buying Creoles. We cannot say for certain that those new slaves described as 'Ebboes' were actually Ibos, or Igbos, from present-day Nigeria, or that twenty Gold Coast children he purchased in 1766 were from Ghana. However, we do know that they had suffered the horrendous conditions on the slave ships and that new purchases would have reinforced African customs and beliefs among the existing enslaved community on the plantation.

Usually slave families adopted the newly arrived children who needed three to five years to become 'seasoned', as did adults. In general about one third to nearly one half of imported Africans died during this 'season-

ing' period. Pinney's death rate at less than a quarter was a little better but still represented an appalling loss of life. During Pero's time on Nevis, the dead would have been buried according to African customs and with African rites, some probably under-

The wooden house at Mountravers
References in Pinney's letters suggest that in his time it was not substantially different to the house in this photograph of about 1903.

Country houses on St Kitts, ca. early twentieth century
Eyewitness accounts of slave housing on Nevis described 'thatched and wattled' houses with two rooms. 'The cabins on which they sleep are a kind of raised benches, made of boards, on which they spread their mats and blankets.'

neath or close to the huts, others in land set aside for the purpose.

We do not know whether Pero lived in Pinney's house or in the slave village. On plantations domestics sometimes slept on the floor or anywhere in the house they could find a quiet spot, and Pero may well have

done so. Pinney gave a general description of the houses on the island in a letter written to a friend in April 1766:

The houses are all built of wood, the kitchen and offices separate, the roof within side are entirely bear (sic), many not even painted. In short they are nothing but shells, therefore

Surface finds from the slave village at Mountravers
In 1998 Channel 4's Time Team mounted an archaeological investigation which focussed on locating the slave village at Mountravers. Also investigated were the remains of the house where Pero was a servant.

you must conceive how odd they appeared to me at first sight. We are pestered in our houses with many disagreeable insects, such as flyes, cock roch's, scorpions, centipedes etc the two last are venomous.[14]

In the slave village families built their own thatched African-style huts of wattle and daub, while single slaves may have lived in segregated dormitory-style housing. The huts were dark, prone to catch fire, and easily damaged by hurricanes and rain. In the 1790s Pinney instructed houses to be 'built at approximate distances in right lines to prevent accidents from fire and to afford each negro a proper piece of land round the house'. In the adjacent yard they had their own garden, with fruit trees and pens for fowls and small animals. In addition, they grew vegetables in provision grounds higher up on the mountain. There they worked on Sundays, their only 'free' day. Even though Pero was a domestic slave with access to food in the plantation house and with a certain amount of status, he would also have grown his own produce to supplement the plantation allowances of salted herrings, corn, potatoes, rice and yams.

It is possible that Pero would have been branded as a very young child, but unlikely that Pinney branded him again although Pinney did own a set of silver negro-brand-

Necklock

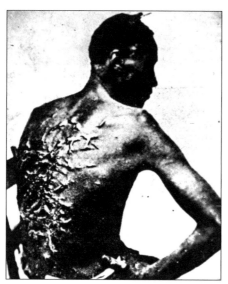

The results of whipping
This image, published in *Harper's Weekly* in 1863, was mass-produced during the American Civil War. On Nevis, magistrates could impose up to 39 lashes for certain offences but planters, who had full power of corporal punishment, often ignored this.

ing marks bought from his 'worthy friend Mr Peter Eaton' in Bristol.[15] At least one known runaway, Polydore, a 'Mina negro', was branded on his left and right breast with Pinney's marks and the date '1766'. Hunters were sent after runaways, some of whom, if caught, were fettered to a block of wood. Pinney paid out over thirty cash rewards for catching runaways during the 18 years Pero worked on Nevis but we do not know whether Pero ever tried to escape. On a small island like Nevis it was difficult to hide but, even so, it is likely that he, too, absented himself to visit family and friends; it was common on plantations for slaves to stay away for a few days and then return of their own accord. Undoubtedly on 'coming home', as Pinney put it, they faced a serious flogging for their transgression. Whips were used on Mountravers, and on 21 February 1767, the same day Pinney purchased a group of nine Ebboe children, he bought six 'negro necklocks'.

Within the context of the time, and of plantation slavery – a system that relied on fierce punishment to control a slave population that vastly outnumbered whites – Pinney's regime may have been less harsh than that of some other planters on Nevis but life on Mountravers was still brutal – more so for the field slaves than the domestic slaves.

Life on Mountravers

PERO WAS NOT the only male servant on Mountravers. Pinney had brought with him from England a white indentured servant, a ten-year-old Dorset boy, Tom Peaden, whom he took on brief visits to England in 1767 and 1774. There is no account of how the work was divided between the boys but by 1771 Tom was an overseer on the plantation and Pero a skilled barber. During part of the sixteen months it took Daniel Martin to teach him 'to Shave and Dress Hair', Pero was boarded out to him, and the training, which ended in December 1768, cost Pinney over N£20. Daniel Martin probably was a white Creole in his late twenties.

Pero's sister Nancy was also taught a trade. Aged about 13, she received from John Pinney N24s:9d for 'learning to darn at St Kitts'.[16] On the same day in July 1770 he also gave Pero N£1:6s:6d, perhaps to accompany Nancy to St Kitts. Miss Janet Weekes was paid 'for Nancy Jones' schooling', which probably also included instruction in domestic duties.

Perhaps Pinney intended Nancy as his future wife's servant; in the late 1760s he was thinking about getting married and entertained many guests at Mountravers. We can assume that Pero received 'tips' from visitors to the house in the same way that Pinney tipped 'Mrs Cottle's and Mr Maynard's

negroes', and 'Mrs Stanley's servants'. Pero was trusted with what would have been large amounts of money for enslaved people: in

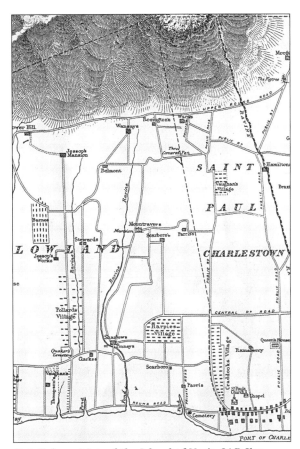

Detail from *Map of the Island of Nevis*, JAB Iles, 1871, showing Mountravers and the surrounding plantations.

one instance he delivered N£28 in cash. Travelling around was a risky undertaking for a young male slave, particularly between islands. He might have been kidnapped, or mistaken for a runaway and taken to jail. In the 1770s two young men from Mountravers were stolen off the island.

Nevis drogher
These lighters were used to land goods from, and load sugar onto, ships lying off-shore, and also for inter-island shipping.

John Pinney,
signed Maynard,
date unclear
The portrait may
show Pinney in
his mid thirties
when he was in
England in 1774
with his servant
Tom Peaden.

A planter family's servant

PINNEY MARRIED Jane Weekes, the daughter of a Nevis planter, on 14 June 1772, and a month later the couple went on their honeymoon, taking Pero and Nancy as servants. On the schooner *Gull* they sailed to Philadelphia, the capital of Pennsylvania, arrived on Friday evening, 14 August 1772, and took lodgings at Mrs Graydon's in Walnut Street. Many distinguished people, the gentry and British officers, frequented Widow Graydon's fashionable boarding house in the centre of town.

Philadelphia, with its large Quaker population, was one of the centres of debate about the abolition of slavery in North America, and, indeed, in 1780 the state did introduce a limited form of abolition. Quakers were persecuted in the West Indies for refusing to bear arms and for trying to convert slaves to Christianity, but in the city's streets Pero and Nancy would have heard Quaker views expressed freely.

Reports of severe hurricane damage on Nevis cut short the visit, and the party left America on 8 November on the brig *Boston*. In his 'Philadelphia voyage account' Pinney accounted for N£218:19s:0d, including passage, 'for my family expenses'. It is likely that the costs of Pero and Nancy were part of these since in a later account Pinney described his servants as 'family', which was quite typical for that period. On his return to Nevis, Pero probably found his living quarters had been destroyed by the hurricane.

Between 1773 and 1781 five Pinney children were born. The arrival of all these children would have brought many changes to the household, and perhaps to Pero's duties. Pero himself became an uncle on 26 April 1775 when his 18-year-old sister Nancy had a mulatto[17] son, William Fisher, who became a playfellow of the Pinney children. The boy's father was white and, like most mulatto children on the plantation, William was taught a trade rather than to work in the fields.

In 1776 Pero learnt to draw teeth, a service often performed by barbers, from a man called Mial who probably was one of the slaves belonging to Pinney's mother-in-law. Pinney did not account for any income derived from Pero's new dentistry skills but it is possible that Pero was able to earn some extra money for himself; tooth decay was rife among the slaves. During the harvest period they were expected to supplement their diet by sucking sugar cane and drinking cane juice. A few years after learning to pull teeth, Pero himself had a tooth extracted. This is the only known record of any medical attention he received and provides the only pointer as to his appearance: perhaps he had a visible gap between his teeth.

Like other enterprising slaves, Pero bought goods from, and sold produce to, his owner. During the 1770s and early 1780s he sold a sheep to Pinney, for N£2:5s:0d, and a goat for N£1:4s:9d. He received payment of N9s for providing three dozen baskets for carrying dung and N12s for a barrow. For a short period Pero himself hired an old enslaved woman, Soone, from Pinney. He paid N6s:12d, but we do not know what work she did for him. This is not the only record of one slave hiring another: in the mid-1790s his sister Nancy was on long-term hire to Mulatto Polly who had been the Pinney children's nurse.

Colonial struggle

PERO SURVIVED the increasing distress and hardships caused by the American War of Independence (1775-1783) in which France joined America against Britain. Nevis was much affected by the war: the French and British attacked each other's valuable West Indian 'possessions', sea battles took place all over the Caribbean and, two years into the war, Pinney wrote excitedly that there were 'Enemies all around us! While at breakfast … I saw a Brig taken, bound to St Christopher, near my own landing.' They were all 'subject to be pilfered and robed (sic) by Pirates in the Night', and he obtained permission to raise a battery of three guns at the foot of his estate, on Pinney's Beach. Slaves kept a nightly watch at 'Fort Pinney' – an additional duty that must have been particularly arduous during crop time.

Nevis planters depended to a large extent on imported foodstuffs, particularly from America, to feed their slaves, and the war disrupted the supply lines, making food very expensive and at times unavailable. By March 1778, 300 to 400 slaves had died from hunger on Nevis and an equal number on St Kitts. It seems that Pinney managed to stave off famine on Mountravers by planting some additional food crops at the expense of sugar cane.

While the Americans fought to free themselves from British colonial rule, enslaved people in the Caribbean continued their fight for freedom. In the spring of 1778 a plot for a slave rebellion was discovered on St Kitts; the slaves aimed 'to deliver the island to the French, or any persons who would make them free'.

On 9 January 1782 the French fleet appeared off Nevis, led by their commander Compte de Grasse. In a show of strength, the next day the fleet passed within range of the capital's rickety and totally insufficient defences and sailed on to St Kitts, where they landed 7,000 French troops. The Nevis Island Council debated what to do. Two of its members, Pinney and James Tobin (who later became his business partner in Bristol) proposed a motion to surrender the island. This they did, on 14 January, on board the French flagship, the *Ville de Paris*. It is quite probable that Pero was present on that occasion. He certainly accompanied Mrs Pinney's father, William Burt Weekes, on a visit to the *Ville de Paris* soon after the surrender. As well as being a planter, Weekes was Treasurer of Nevis and Captain Gunner of the forts and in that capacity would have negotiated the handover of the island's defences.

Meanwhile, St Kitts had not surrendered. On 22 January the British fleet appeared from Antigua, also sailed past Nevis, and three days later engaged the French in the Battle of

The Close of the Battle of the Saints, Nicholas Pocock, ca. 1782
On 12 April 1782 Admiral de Grasse was forced to surrender his flagship, the *Ville de Paris*, in the Battle of the Saints off Dominica. Taken as a prize and badly damaged, she and her crew were lost in a gale off Newfoundland. The Admiral was not on board and the French pilloried him, later, for having lost the battle.

Frigate Bay. 'Nevis residents climbed into the hills'[18] to watch this spectacular and bloody event, and there would certainly have been an excellent view from the Pinney house at Mountravers. Although the battle forced the French to withdraw from Frigate Bay, it did not stop them from taking St Kitts. Later, in April, they departed from Martinique on an expedition against Jamaica, again led by de Grasse and the *Ville de Paris*.

Two freed slave women

PINNEY HAD ALWAYS intended his stay on Nevis to be a temporary one but plantation affairs and the American War of Independence delayed his departure. Pero would have known about his master's desire to leave the West Indies and one may guess how he suffered from conflicting emotions about this prospect and the uncertainty about his future. However, Pero was not the first black person to leave Nevis for England.

In 1778 Pinney sent his oldest son John Frederick to England, followed in April 1781 by his children Elizabeth (Betsey) and Azariah 'under the care' of the 'negro woman servant' Kate Coker. She was obviously trusted to deliver the two young children safely to England. After a brief stay in London with various planter families from Nevis they travelled to Woodcutts, in East Dorset, the home of Pinney's plantation manager, and Kate's previous owner, William Coker.

This was Kate's second visit to England; in 1777 she had accompanied a captain's wife as her servant. After returning to Nevis, Kate had started buying her own freedom, probably with the proceeds from her trip to England. Although she had not been able to pay the full purchase price due to being ill and unable to work, she was freed, or manumitted, in September 1778. After Kate's return to Nevis in 1781 she began to buy the freedom of her mother, Catherine, who was mortgaged to Pinney by his father-in-law, William Burt Weekes. Catherine died before the sale could be completed.

Kate was manumitted on the same day as the eleven-year-old Fanny Coker who had been christened as a four-year-old and trained as a seamstress in the mid-1770s. After being freed, Fanny remained in the Pinney household. It is believed that William Coker was her father. Her mother was Black Polly, an 'Ebboe', who was the first girl Pinney had bought soon after his arrival on Nevis. Black Polly always maintained that her mulatto son William Jones, born in January 1773, was Pinney's child but he strenuously denied this.

Woodcutts Farm, the Dorset family home of John Pinney's
relative and plantation manager William Coker
Kate Coker stayed at Woodcutts in 1781 and again in 1785.
Pero and Fanny Coker stayed there in 1783.

Arriving in a 'free country', but still a slave

JUST BEFORE finally leaving for England in 1783, Pinney valued all his 193 slaves but not the 30-year-old Pero. Pinney noted simply that he was 'to go with me to England'. Pero, his sisters and Harriott had turned out to be a good investment: Sheeba was worth N£100, Nancy N£90 and Harriott N£60. Even without Pero, the three women were now worth a quarter more than the original purchase price for the whole group.

On 5 July 1783, 18 years almost to the day since Pinney had bought him, Pero left Nevis. He sailed with Mr and Mrs Pinney, their baby son Pretor, and Fanny Coker, now Mrs Pinney's maid, and after a journey of 41 days on the *Jonge Vrow Charlotte* they arrived off Dover on 15 August 1783.

For a short while, Pero, Fanny Coker and Mrs Pinney stayed in London while John Pinney travelled to Coker's house at Woodcutts in Dorset. During their first few months Pero and Fanny probably felt a mixture of culture shock and excitement. They may well have met in their masters' houses or at inns other slaves or freed people, taken as servants from the West Indies. London's black population was perhaps about the size of the whole population of Nevis, and black people were a common feature of London life where the majority were not slaves but free people working in a variety of jobs.

It is likely that the two newcomers knew of newspaper articles accusing black servants of taking the jobs of white English people. In 1764 the *Gentleman's Magazine* complained that arriving in England black people 'cease to consider themselves as slaves in this free country, nor will they put up with an inequality in treatment'.[19] However, it is worth remembering that in this 'free country' Pero was still enslaved. The famous court ruling in 1772 by Judge Mansfield had only established that slaves could not be compelled to return to the West Indies; they could still be bought and sold in England and runaways pursued by slave hunters. When in 1790 'a black woman was hunted down in the Bristol streets and dragged to the ship that was to take her to the West Indies',[20] the pursuit was lawful but taking her outside the country against her will was not. Pero could only have achieved complete freedom by manumission, and he must have hoped that he would be freed if he behaved to his master's satisfaction but there appears to be no evidence that he ever was.

Pero had arrived in England during the summer but by now it was autumn. Before leaving London he was bought a new pair of boots costing £1:3s:0d. On 6 November 1783 Mrs Pinney, Pero and Fanny set off for deepest rural Dorset where they spent Christmas at Woodcutts with the Cokers. Pero got a

Advertisement
Felix Farley's Bristol Journal, 9 January 1768

present of 10 shillings, the same amount as Pinney's children but twice as much as Fanny. After Christmas the Pinneys and their servants temporarily moved to Salisbury and then, at the beginning of February 1784, to Bath.

BEFORE LEAVING NEVIS, Pinney had decided to settle in Bristol rather than London. He chose Bristol because the air was cleaner, life in the city cheaper and there were better business opportunities. On 16 March 1784 Pinney moved his family and servants to Bristol where he set up in business as a sugar factor with his friend from Nevis, the pro-slave trade campaigner James Tobin.

Shortly after the move Pinney penned a memo to himself that he would reserve the sum of £1,500 owed to him in the West Indies 'to purchase a House in the airy part of Bristol, or elsewhere, for my residence'. In the meantime family and servants lived in a rented house at No. 5 Park Street.

Both Pero and Fanny would have found the household run on much more formal lines than was common in the West Indies where, as a contemporary observer wrote, 'no servants are in waiting to announce arrivals; visitors, negroes, dogs, cats, poultry, all walk in and out, and up and down your rooms, without the slightest ceremony'.[21]

In contrast to the number of times Fanny is mentioned in the Pinney Papers, the references to Pero become fewer from 1786 onwards. The only time we ever actually catch a glimpse of him and hear his voice is in a letter Pinney wrote about a visit to Park Street by his former plantation manager, the alcoholic Joseph Gill in July 1786:

As my servant Pero was standing by the door, he walked up and enquired for me, who told him I was out, gone to the exchange, but his Mistress was upstairs, he desired him to walk into the parlour which he declined, leaving his compliments for Mrs P – and saying if he should not see me there, he would call in the afternoon: Since which I have not heard from him but yesterday, by accident, I heard that he lodged at the Whitehart Inn in Broad Street and intended London in a few days. Pero observed that he was dressed shabbily, in an old flaped (sic) hat, and a Coat with a hole in its back, his face appeared much swelled.

By contrast, Pinney would have wanted Pero to look smart and, indeed, had ordered cloth for his servants' liveries soon after moving to Park Street. It was customary for senior servants of distinguished households to wear wigs but it is unlikely that Pero would have been made to wear a padlocked metal collar, made of brass, copper or silver, and inscribed with the owner's name and coat of arms, or other such detail. The collars probably had gone out of fashion, and anyway, Pinney would have considered them too ostentatious. He may well, also, have trusted Pero not to run away.

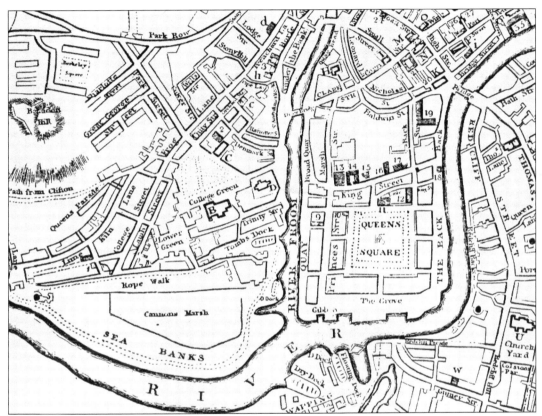

Detail from *Mathews's New & Correct Plan of the City and Suburbs of Bristol,* **1794**
This shows Great George Street three years after Pero and Fanny Coker moved into the
Georgian House.

GENTLEMEN rarely went anywhere without their personal attendants, and it is likely that the well-travelled Pero accompanied Pinney on a journey to Paris in September and October 1789. These were dangerous times: only two months earlier the Bastille had been stormed in Paris, triggering unrest all over France. The villages had restructured themselves into self-governing communes, the country was still unstable, and travelling must have been hazardous.

Mrs Pinney was ill during Pinney's absence. She suffered from gallstones and fevers and planned to recover her health on Nevis. Although Fanny was her personal servant and companion, she initially refused to go but, threatened with dismissal, she sailed with her mistress from Bristol in November 1789 on the *Union Island*. Pinney railed against Fanny's 'ungrateful conduct' and 'unaccountable behaviour and cruelty', but four months later she and Pero were the only servants retained when he, with Pero, also left for Nevis, arriving on 30 April 1790. This was the first time in seven years Pero or Fanny had seen their families. Fanny saw for the first time her five-year-old brother Cubbenna and two-year-old sister, Little Molly, and one can imagine their families' joy on their return.

During their visit, the neighbouring planter John Latoysonere Scarborough bought his three 'mestize'[22] children from Pinney and freed them soon after. Their mother was Mulatto Polly, the former nurse of Pinney's children.

Pinney took to England Mulatto Polly's oldest daughter, the ten-year-old Christianna

Jane Weekes,
Mrs Pinney, daughter of a Nevis planter

A View of Nevis from St Kitts, **Nicholas Pocock, 1790**
Commissioned by Pinney, Pocock's romantic, idealised image has no reference to slavery and bears little resemblance to the actual landscape although he had sailed to the West Indies several times in the 1770s, and his last trip in the snow *Minerva* was to Nevis.

Jacques, who was also described as a 'mestize', indicating that her father, too, was white. It appears that Pinney did not pay her passage on board his ship, the *Nevis*, and she may not have been part of his household. They all arrived on the evening of 11 September 1790 at Lamplighter's Hall, in Shirehampton on the river Avon. Interestingly, in the accounts for the 1790 Nevis trip Pinney used Pero's aliases of 'William Jones' and 'Pero Jones' more frequently than usual. It was as if during that trip Pero was a whole person, a man with a family and a family name.

A couple of years before going to Nevis, Pinney had sent out some sundry articles on Pero's behalf. Mrs Pinney's aunt was to sell them on the island, and immediately after their return Pero and Fanny began shipping various presents, and goods that could be sold – an early form of remittance where West Indians supported their families back home. On 31 October 1790 Pero sent parcels, 'one for his Father one for his sister one for Bridget', a parcel for his nephew William Fisher and two for another slave. Bridget was the mother of Tom Peaden's daughter, and Pero sending her a parcel suggests a friendly relationship. In the same shipment Fanny sent 'a handkerchief' [head wrap] for Nanny Weekes who probably was a friend of hers. The exchange of produce and presents was a two-way traffic: on his second visit to Nevis, Pero brought back with him a 'small keg of sugar and a small bundle', a gift from a woman to her daughter who lived in Dorset. It was 'packed up just as it was delivered by her to Pero, as he supposed there might be some money inclosed (sic) in it …'. Having secured it with an extra wrapper, Pinney's father-in-law sent on the presents via William Coker at Woodcutts.

Since Pinney's own ships travelled back and forth to Nevis, they not only carried gifts and goods but would also have kept Pero and Fanny supplied with news from their families.

Moving to Great George Street

IN 1788 WORK had started on Pinney's new house in Great George Street but on returning from Nevis, he found that it was not completed. After staying for a few weeks with James Tobin and family, the Pinneys and servants took lodgings in Albemarle Row, Clifton, until they moved, in 1791, into what is now 7 Great George Street, Bristol's Georgian House Museum.

As yet, it is not known where Pero and Fanny Coker lived in the house. There are five servants' rooms in the attic, and it is possible that Pero or Fanny (as senior staff) each had one of these. In contrast to the comfortable and beautifully decorated rooms their masters occupied, the servants' rooms would have been very plain and sparsely furnished with cast-off furniture. At Racedown, one of Pinney's Dorset houses, the 'Men Servants Chamber Attick' had a 'stump Bedstead', a bed and bolster, an arm chair and a 'Perambulator Case' – presumably for a child's pram – while the maid's room also had two chairs, one of which was broken, three 'best Whitby Blankets' and one 'Old Blanket', as well as a 'Yellow Ware Chamber Pot'.

Pero and Fanny certainly ate with the servants. The Pinneys regularly ordered from their plantation managers 'yellow Guht plums' (probably mangoes), ginger, guava marmalade and jelly, tamarinds, pineapples, pickled peppers, yams, cassava bread, sugar and rum for their own use, and turtles for special occasions. No doubt the servants would at least have had the leftovers from this West Indian table.

As the valet, Pero should have been the head of the male servants in the house. Although he had served Pinney far longer than any of the others, this privilege might have been denied him because he was black and a slave.

Pinney's house in Great George Street, the Georgian House
The dormer window of the servants' quarters in the attic can just be seen behind the tree.

Study in the Georgian House
From here Pinney conducted business including the purchase and sale of slaves on Nevis.

Pero and Fanny were the most constant members of the Pinney servant 'family', and they worked alongside other servants who came and went. Among these, at various times, were Sarah Marks, an 'upper servant'; Mary Chaplin, the cook; Charles Thomas, a footman; David Williams, a coachman; and Ann Roberts, perhaps a housemaid. The Pinneys also had a gardener and a woman who came in to do the washing.

There is no record of Pero's duties in the house. As Pinney's personal servant he would have been on hand at all hours and performed the usual tasks of a valet: shaving his master in the mornings, powdering his wig, looking after his hair, helping him dress and undress, waiting at table and performing other duties around the house. He paid for items and services during Pinney's absence, for instance 10 shillings coach hire for the family while Pinney was away in Dorset in March 1795. Pero rode a horse; Pinney wanted him to take some goods from Bristol to Dorset 'in a Portmanteau behind him', and as a literate man Pero would have been particularly useful in running business errands.

The black servant community in Bristol

ALTHOUGH THE EARLIEST RECORD of an African servant in Bristol is of Sir John Young's 'black moore' gardener in about 1560, there is no evidence of significant numbers of black people living in the city during the sixteenth and seventeenth centuries. However, given that black servants were regarded as a status symbol and many West Indian planters, merchants and captains brought with them slaves and freed slaves, by Pero's time there must have been a sizeable black population in Bristol, as well as a scatter of black people in country houses, villages and small towns all over the West Country. The exact size of the black population at that time will never be known but in the early 1770s it was suggested that there were 14,000 or 15,000 black people in the whole country.[23] The majority were said to have lived in London, and the rest mainly in the slaving ports of Liverpool and Bristol.

Their presence is evident from references in parish registers and newspapers, and occasional grave markers, such as those of Scipio Africanus, in Henbury churchyard, and Samuel Thompson, in St Andrew's cemetery, Clifton.

Unlike today, when Bristol's black population is mainly of Jamaican origin, black people in eighteenth-century Bristol would have come from all over the West Indies and North America, reflecting the diverse business interests of the city's planters and merchants. From the Pinney Papers and other sources it is possible to document a small community of black people who came from Nevis. Those associated with Pinney's business partner James Tobin and his family illustrate the connections: Pero and Fanny Coker would have known well George Evans and Priscilla Gould, Tobin's servants who lived just up the road in Berkeley Square. They

Bristol Cathedral and College Green from Great George Street, Thomas L Rowbotham, 1827
The view could almost have been taken from the Pinney family drawing room.

Miniature of James Tobin, artist unknown, ca. 1790
Pinney's friend and business partner, Tobin, wrote a series of pamphlets attacking the abolitionist James Ramsay.

may also have known Tobin's half-sister Ann who was living in Bristol in 1780. Tobin's father-in-law, George Webbe senior, had a black servant at his house in Redland, and his brother-in-law, George Webbe junior, brought his servant John Pierre from Falmouth on visits to Bristol. Fanny Coker would have known Charles Hamilton, a free man from Kingston, Jamaica, who had been unlawfully taken to St Kitts. His freedom was only restored by the intervention of the courts there, and in 1815 he was brought as a freeman from Nevis to Bristol by Tobin's daughter-in-law, Jane.

There were certainly other black servants with Bristol families who had substantial links with the West Indies, such as the Bushes, Cobhams, and Baillies. In addition, there were frequent visitors from the Caribbean:

those who were taken by their masters, and those who travelled as free black people. Kate Coker, for instance, was back in England in June 1785 on her third transatlantic trip. Employed as a servant, she accompanied Mrs Jones, a Nevis minister's wife, and her daughter Sarah to England. During her time in Bristol Kate Coker stayed with them in their lodgings in King Street, with the widow of a ship's captain who had died recently on a voyage from Nevis.[24] Kate Coker returned to the West Indies in November on the *Resolution*, together with several planters and their children.

Nanny Weekes, to whom Fanny Coker had sent a present of a headscarf, came to Bristol in 1797. She had recently been freed by Mrs Pinney's aunt and travelled from Nevis to deliver the orphaned sons of Mrs Pinney's half-brother. Pinney had expressly requested that 'no Negroe, or Servant' should accompany the two boys as there had already been 'too much communication with the inhabitants of this country' and he feared 'that the Colonies ... experience the consequence of such intercourse'. He undoubtedly was afraid that the travellers would return to Nevis with seditious ideas of freedom, spreading unrest on the island.

Frances (Fanny) Coker and Christianna Jacques

FANNY COKER'S status in the Pinney household was different from Pero's. Although she had been a slave, she was a free woman, and a 'mulatto'. According to Pinney, she had been brought up by Mrs Pinney 'with great Tenderness, and we have never considered her in the light of a menial servant, but as one who had a claim to our protection and support'. Fanny was a longstanding member of Broadmead Baptist Church but it is not known whether Pero, or other black slave-servants, also attended this congregation.

Fanny's duties were those of a lady's maid but she was also Mrs Pinney's constant companion. There are numerous references from a later period to her accompanying her mistress to the Pinney's country house at Somerton, and to Exmouth, Weymouth and London. Unlike Pero she was paid a regular wage, £10 a year in 1793. She received less than the 'upper servant' Sarah Marks, who got £12:12s:0d, and more than the housemaid. Like Pero, Fanny was literate. On Nevis she had been schooled with two of Pinney's children.

Christianna's story during this period is not clear. When she arrived in Bristol in September 1790, she was a ten-year-old slave girl, overwhelmed by the whole experience. Pinney quickly wrote to his manager to impress upon her mother, Mulatto Polly, that he

would be obliged to send her home 'as it is inconceivable how ill she behaves for such a child'. Although it is possible that she may have been a slave-servant in the house, it is more likely that she worked for one of Pinney's connections in Bristol. In 1797 Pinney freed her mother, Mulatto Polly, and Christianna's young sisters Peggy and Nancy. Mulatto Polly then paid ten guineas a year 'to furnish her daughter Christianna with clothes and washing' during a three-year apprenticeship, and references in the account books suggest that Christianna was apprenticed to a seamstress. Later on she visited the Georgian House and ate with the cook. She seems to have been a strong-willed young woman whose behaviour caused Pinney some anxiety. He wrote that 'if Christianna behaves well she will likewise have her freedom, but I hope she will never return to the West Indies'.

In 1806 Christianna was still in England and appears to have been living in Chatham, Kent, at the time her mother came to Bristol. Mulatto Polly had accompanied the planter William Scarborough and his wife as a servant on their journey from Nevis. The couple stayed in Lyme Regis and were unwilling to pay for her passage home, so Mulatto Polly came to Bristol. Pinney appealed to Mr Scarborough for the money as the 'poor Woman ... was much distressed for want of

Dining room in the Georgian House

it and her Daughter who came to see her from Chatham'. Mulatto Polly, clearly a woman of some substance who used the visits as opportunities for trading, made the journey from Nevis to Bristol at least twice more.

The main kitchen in the Georgian House

Another visit to Nevis

DURING A VISIT to Racedown, which Joseph Gill now managed, Pero scalded his leg and was unable to walk. While Mrs Pinney and her father left by the Bridport chaise, Gill – lonely, homesick for the West Indies and still drinking too much – could enjoy Pero's company a few days longer until he was fit enough to follow on horseback. Gill, no doubt, would have given Pero a present or some money to take to Nevis for his former mistress, Penny Markham, whom he had freed after his return to England.

Six weeks after this accident, just after Christmas 1793, Pero left Bristol for a short trip to the West Indies with Pinney and his eldest son, John Frederick. Despite the war with France, which had broken out ten months before, the travellers were hoping for a speedy voyage. Instead, Pinney's ship, the *Nevis*, was stuck in Cork, having to wait for a convoy to safeguard passage across the Atlantic. They finally left on 22 March on the *Nevis*, captained by Charles Maies whose hired 'negroe boy servant' sometimes trav-

Bristol Harbour with the Cathedral and Quay, **Nicholas Pocock, 1785,** possibly commissioned by Thomas Daniel, a merchant and ship owner with substantial West India interests.

elled with him. Pero may well have had the company of this young man, or other black people on the voyage. Not only women travelled to Europe as servants: on one ship there was a 'Negroe Lad passenger who is free and who went out last year as a hired servant to attend to a Gentleman on his passage'.

The *Nevis* arrived on 8 May 1794, having sailed via Carlisle Bay (Barbados), Port Royal and St Pierre (Martinique). Both Barbados and Martinique had recently been at the centre of naval engagements between British and French fleets: at the beginning of February General Charles Gray had set sail from Barbados for French possessions, and Martinique had surrendered after its Royal Fort

fell towards the end of the month. By June a great part of the French West Indian empire lay in British hands.

The party visited Martinique briefly, for Pinney's son wrote that it 'is a fine and fruitful island, and has many resources within itself which renders it as pleasant as any European country. There are various European Amusements and Mechanicks of all descriptions...'.

How Pero and the Pinneys were received on Nevis after their lengthy voyage and what state the plantation was in was not recorded, except that 'Our arrival at Nevis was much looked for'. Frustratingly, Pinney never described his estate or its people in those letters

Mountravers
Seen from the neighbouring Clarke's plantation.

that survive, preferring, on this occasion, to record in detail his anger at what he regarded as the wasteful behaviour of his manager. His son was no more enlightening in his correspondence. The one known visitor to Mountravers in 1800, Tom Wedgwood, did not document the estate, either, or its daily activities. His only observation of life around him came at the end of a letter which referred lyrically to 'birds singing on all sides of me – oranges by thousands close to the house – a supper on land-crabs …'. [25]

The long delay at the beginning of the 1794 trip meant that the visitors from Bristol could only stay for a couple of months if they were to avoid sailing during the middle of the hurricane season. They left Nevis on 30 July, the day Christianna's sister Peggy was born. Pinney wrote that on their return journey on the *Nevis* they 'had a very tempestuous passage, and from the 25th of August, when we were separated from the convoy, to the 19th [of September] the day we arrived [at King Road, near Portishead], we remained without a single sail in company but thank God we not only escaped the dangers of the sea but also of the enemy'. They finally set foot on dry land at Lamplighters Hall and took a coach home from there. The convoy had arrived before the *Nevis* and this delay, and a 'perfect storm', caused Mrs Pinney to have 'high hysteric fits' until the travellers came home at 7 o'clock in the evening.

During this voyage Pero was 'obliged … to pay constant attention' to a turtle Pinney had brought from Nevis. A month after their return the animal was sent to Thomas Wyndham MP, at Dunravon Castle in Glamorganshire, 'properly placed in a Basket made for the purpose'. In Nevis, turtles were placed in special 'crawls' but it is not known where they were kept in Bristol.

Detail of *View of the Avon at Hotwells, Bristol with the Clifton Suspension Bridge and the Paddle Steamer 'Wye', Samuel Jackson ca. 1836*
Turtles, a popular luxury food in Georgian Britain, were often sent as presents from Nevis, even well into the 1850s. Many died on the voyage, or after being landed.

Years of decline

THERE IS SOME circumstantial evidence in the plantation slave lists that suggests Pero had one, or possibly two, daughters, born after he left Nevis. This, and the separation from his family, may explain Pero's decline. He may have been depressed by his personal circumstances, or angry about the continuing slave trade and the conditions his fellow slaves had to endure.[26]

Whatever caused Pero's deterioration, Pinney later wrote about him that 'almost ever since we left Nevis in 1794 his conduct has been very reprehensible – insomuch, that his Mistress and every branch of my Family have urged me to discharge him and to send him back to Nevis with an annual allowance; provided his behaviour there should have deserved it'.

The concept of 'deserving' and 'undeserving' was central to Pinney's relationships, and presumably he judged that his servant's behaviour did not deserve the reward of being freed and being pensioned off. Perhaps Pinney just feared that Pero would drink himself to death in no time but it is likely that he also feared his destabilising influence on the slave population. After all, in his life of somewhat privileged dependency, Pero had enjoyed a certain freedom of movement, had acquired some wealth and had benefited from a small degree of autonomy that was denied plantation slaves. Whatever the reasons, Pero remained in Bristol, presumably increasingly unhappy with his situation. He may have rebelled by withdrawing his labour and not performing his duties to his master's satisfaction for Pinney later wrote that Pero 'became so great a lover of liquor and connected with such abandoned characters, that we could not depend upon him a moment'. The people Pinney described as 'abandoned characters' may of course have been fugitive slaves and abolitionists.

Pero would have seen deals being struck in the study of the Georgian House between Pinney and other planters, involving the recovery and sale of slaves as mortgaged property. At the same time, he would also have known from various sources, including the local black community in Bristol, about the debates taking place in Parliament and in the newspapers over the abolition of the slave trade. He would have heard about the great Slave Revolt on Haiti and, surely, would have approved of the ideas of 'liberty, equality and fraternity' spread by the French Revolution. No doubt, Pero would have read Olaudah Equiano's brilliant, passionate review of two pro-slavery pamphlets published by James Tobin, in which he accused Tobin of 'unrelenting barbarity', and of being a 'malicious slanderer', 'deserving a flagellation' himself.[27] At Great George Street

Possible 'slave dungeon' at Mountravers
This early twentieth century photograph may show the Mountravers jail. Many estates had such lock-up rooms although sometimes the planta- tion hospital, or sick-house, was used. Nevis planters were largely free to discipline their slaves as they saw fit although legally they were not per- mitted to mutilate or kill as punishment.

Pero certainly would have met people with abolitionist sympathies, such as William Wordsworth, who stayed with the Pinneys for five weeks in August and September 1795, and, most likely, the poets Southey and Coleridge together with others in that circle.

Although, rather dramatically, Pinney wrote 'that we could not depend upon him a moment', in the summer of 1796 Pero was charged with some of the travel arrange- ments on a journey to Derbyshire. He and Fanny Coker accompanied Mrs Pinney, John Frederick and Betsey, who wrote to her father:

We arrived at Gloucester on Wednesday at three o'clock – Pero came to the Inn only a few minutes before us – we therefore could not send him to Cheltenham for an hour or two, on account of the horse – he sat off (sic) at 5 o'clock and our coachman brought the horses to us at nine o'clock that night we therefore thought it the wisest plan to remain at Gloucester that night and proceed to Cheltenham the next morning.

While Pero rode on horseback, Mrs Pinney, her children and Fanny travelled 'in the curricule'.

Cheltenham was 'very full and company coming in every day' but Buxton proved so expensive that the visit was cut short. While Mrs Pinney complained about the cost of their beds, she was relieved that 'the men servants we pay nothing for' – presumably Pero and the coachman slept on the floor in the stable or in the kitchen of the inn they were staying at. The party swiftly moved on to Lichfield and Matlock.

We get another glimpse of Pero in December 1796, when he attended the funeral of Mrs Pinney's father. William Burt Weekes was buried in Wraxall, near Bristol, and Pinney wrote that '... the hearse, a chariott and four Coaches... with my Carriage and servants made up the Procession'.

Pero's death

BY THE END OF MAY 1798 Pero was ill. John Pinney wrote in a letter that all his family were well 'except my Servant Pero who is very ill and now at Ashton for a change of air. I much doubt his recovery – one or other of us visit him three or four times a week. He has waited on my person upward of thirty-two years, and I cannot help feeling much for him, notwithstanding he has not lately conducted himself as well as I could have wished'. It is likely that Pero was in the household of Robert Bush at Ashton Lodge, in the parish of Cold Ashton, Gloucestershire. Set in the upland edge of the Cotswolds, the house, now Battlefields House, was in an excellent situation for a recuperative 'change of air'. There were strong connections between the West India merchant and planter families Pinney, Bush and Tobin, links cemented further by the marriage in 1804 between Robert Bush's son Robert and Tobin's daughter Fanny.

However, the efforts at saving Pero failed and, at the age of about 45, he died some time between May and November 1798 'after being almost useless, caused by drunkenness and dissipation', as Pinney described it. In another letter Pinney wrote curtly to his plantation manager: 'I am very sorry to inform you of the death of Pero, though it was a great relief to himself and us'.

Mrs Pinney distributed Pero's belongings to his family on Nevis. She sent a box of his clothes to be divided between his father and his nephew, William Fisher. She sold his watch and purchased a pair of gold earrings for each of his sisters, Nancy, Eve and Sheeba. Ten guineas he had by him when he died she sent to his family 'with the Earrings, in the tin Case, tied up in different parcels with the names of the Family written on each; to whom it is to be given'. Afterwards Pinney learnt from the servants that Pero had frequently lent money, at interest. However, 'as there is not the smalest (sic) Memo of it amongst his papers, in all probability the money will be lost to the family'. There seems to be no record of any effort by Pinney to make good the loss as a gesture to Pero's family.

So far no records of his burial have been found. He might have been buried near Ashton Lodge, or, bearing in mind his alias of 'William Jones', it is possible that he was buried in Bristol in the graveyard of St. Augustine the Less. The burial register notes the burial of a William Jones on 19 June 1798. Nothing suggests that at any time in his life he was ever a free man.

Pero's Bridge, Bristol Harbourside

What happened to...

Harriott

Harriott, still a slave, 'died suddenly', on 9 July 1801, aged about 60. It is not known whether she had any children.

Nancy Jones and her son, William Fisher

In 1808 Pinney sold Mountravers plantation to Edward Huggins who was known at the time to be cruel to his slaves. However, Pinney had reserved a group of enslaved people to be hired out on his personal account to a neighbouring plantation. Although she was originally reserved by Pinney as one of these, Pinney changed his mind and sold Nancy and her son to Huggins. With eight others, this group of ten people was attached to Woodlands, the upper part of Mountravers, where they also lived. At a height of perhaps 1,200 feet it was much cooler, and therefore healthier, at Woodlands than at lower-lying plantations.

In December 1824 Nancy Jones was sold again, to Mrs Frederick Huggins, the wife of a merchant and blacksmith. A month later Nancy's son William died, aged 49.

Nancy Jones never made it to freedom. On 5 July 1829 she was buried in St Paul's churchyard, Charlestown, where her son had been buried four years earlier. She was said to have been 73 years old and resident in Charlestown.

Sheeba Jones

Unlike her sister Nancy and nephew William Fisher, Sheeba was at no time reserved for hiring out by Pinney.

A field slave in the 1790s, by 1805 Sheeba was doing laundry in the household of the then plantation manager and was said to 'behave very well'. She was sold to Huggins and died between 1831 and 1834, in her early seventies. It is not known whether she had any children.

Kate Coker/Catherine Emra

Kate, later known as Catherine Emra, rented one of Pinney's houses in Charlestown. In 1810 she complained 'that she is obliged to pay rent for land occupied by another person'. As a result she may have withheld payment: the last reference to her was in May 1813, concerning rent arrears.

Christianna Jacques

It is likely that Christianna worked as a seamstress. In the spring of 1803 she was married, probably to a Mr Lewis, and was last heard of in Chatham in 1806. It is not known whether she was ever freed.

Frances (Fanny) Coker

Fanny remained as Mrs Pinney's servant and companion. She acquired some wealth, partly through an annual allowance left by Pinney in his will.

After being nursed for a while, Fanny died in Bristol, unmarried, on 12 April 1820. According to the Baptist records, she had 'lived honourably and died comfortably' and was buried in the Baptist Burial Ground, Redcross Street (now a public park). After the graveyard fell into disuse, the graves were transferred in 1926 to Greenbank Cemetery, Bristol, where a single memorial marks the graves that were moved.

In her will she bequeathed £80, a watch, clothes and other goods to her immediate family on Nevis, and her 'best tea chest' to fellow servant Ann Seymour. (The chest, made of wood, consisted of compartments for different kinds of tea and sugar.) Fanny Coker also left £5 to the Baptist Missionary Society that was doing missionary work in the West Indies and Africa and beginning to address the abolition of slavery.

Although her brother Billey Jones died shortly before Fanny, on Nevis she was survived by her mother, her other siblings and over a dozen nephews and nieces.

Pero's daughters?

It is likely that either Princess or Nanny, or possibly both, were Pero's daughters:

Princess's mother Myrtilla was an African woman, said to have been an 'Ebboe'. Myrtilla's son Hercules had died as a very young child in 1789/90, and she died in childbed, or soon after giving birth to Princess, on 6 January 1795. Myrtilla was around 40 years old.

Princess was originally reserved by Pinney but given up for sale to Huggins and in the same group of ten enslaved people as Nancy Jones and her son. The orphaned girl was almost certainly looked after by her aunt Nancy. By the beginning of 1807 Princess had leprosy. She died some time before December 1816.

Nanny was born on 7 February 1795. Her mother, Richen's Quasheba, a field slave, had two more daughters, Sally and Kitty. Nanny was on the upper plantation, Woodlands, with Princess, Pero's sister and nephew, and six others. At this time her mother and sisters were hired to the neighbouring estate of Clarke's. There her mother died, probably in her fifties, between 1817 and 1822, and then her sister Sally, on 30 March 1830, aged 29. Nanny died a few months later, on 10 Oct 1830, on Mountravers.

Notes

1. 1830 Election placard quoted in Dresser and Giles *Bristol and Transatlantic Slavery* p80.

2. These were mostly poor people from England and Ireland but also convicted criminals, assorted debtors, vagrants and political dissidents. They mortgaged themselves for a number of years of servitude, in return for free passage, food and shelter. If they survived their period of servitude, and fewer than half did, they were free. Thousands of white bonded labourers left from the port of Bristol.

3. Bush *Slave Women in Caribbean Society* p4.

4. Estimates for British vessels range from between 2.6 and 4 million Africans.

5. The well-established practice of African slavery as, however, not based on race, nor did the economy depend entirely on slaves, as it did in the American colonies.

6. Lambert *Sessional Papers* vol 71 p19.

7. Equiano *The Interesting Narrative* p58.

8. Tyson and Highfield *Kamina Folk* p45.

9. Fryer *Staying Power* pp72-3.

10. Ferguson *The History of Mary Prince* p77.

11. Ferguson *The History of Mary Prince* in the Preface by Ziggi Alexander.

12. Fryer *Staying Power* p102.

13. About £5,750 in today's money.

14. The Story of the Bettiscombe Skull, J S Udal, *Dorset Natural History and Antiquarian Field Club*, vol. 3, 1910.

15. Peter Eaton, a 'wholesale grocer', ran his business from 30 Small Street *(Sketchley's Bristol Directory 1775)*. It was Pero who brought news of Eaton's death. On 4 March 1785 Pinney recorded in his journal: 'Pero-Jones, my Servant came from Bristol yesterday, the third, with a letter from Mr James Tobin, advising me of the death of my worthy friend Mr Peter Eaton who died the morning.'

16. The neighbouring island of St Christopher, also known as St Kitts.

17. The child of a black and a white parent.

18. Hubbard *Swords, Ships and Sugar* p146.

19. Fryer *Staying Power* p204.

20. Fryer *Staying Power* p126 and p203.

21. Lewis *Journal of a Residence* p76.

22. The child of a mulatto and a white parent.

23. In the mid-1760s one estimate put the number of black people at 20,000 for London alone but others have seen this as the total for the whole country, while a modern historian has halved that figure.

24. It is likely they were lodging at 36 King Street: in 1775 *Sketchley's Directory* placed Henry Webb, captain of the *Nevis Planter*, at that address.

25. Litchfield *Tom Wedgwood* p90. The sickly son of the abolitionist Josiah Wedgwood and a friend of his children; John Pinney allowed Wedgwood to stay at Mountravers as part of a recuperative voyage to the West Indies in 1800.

26. In the year that Pero died, the Leeward Islands Council and Assembly grudgingly passed the Melioration Act, following a motion in Westminster to improve the situation of slaves in the British colonies. In many instances the legislation was not enforced on Nevis.

27. Equiano's response was published in the *Public Advertiser* on 28 January 1788 and is printed in the Penguin edition of his *Interesting Narrative* pp328-30.

Sources

Pero first came to public attention in Professor Richard Pares's pioneering work on the economic history of the Pinney family, *A West India Fortune* (Longmans, Green & Co, London 1950), and a great debt is owed to this publication.

Most of the information in this book is based on documents in the Pinney Papers, held in the University of Bristol Library, Special Collections. Original sources have also been consulted in the Bristol Record Office, the Public Record Office in London, as well as the archives of the Nevis Historical and Conservation Society and the Government of Nevis in the Court House, Charlestown.

In addition, the following publications have been helpful:

Bush, Barbara *Slave Women in Caribbean Society 1650-1838* Heinemann Publishers (Caribbean), Kingston and James Currey, London 1990

Craton, Michael *Empire Enslavement and Freedom in the Caribbean* Ian Randle, Jamaica, and James Currey, London 1997

Dresser, Madge and Giles, Sue (eds) *Bristol & Transatlantic Slavery* (catalogue of the exhibition 'A Respectable Trade? Bristol & Transatlantic Slavery', 6 March – 2 Sept 1999) Bristol Museum and Art Gallery with the University of the West of England 2000

Eltis, David; Behrend, Stephen D; Richardson, David and Klein, Herbert S (eds) *The Trans-Atlantic Slave Trade* CD-ROM Cambridge University Press 1999

Equiano, Olaudah *The Interesting Narrative and Other Writings* Penguin Books 1995

Ferguson, Moira (ed) *The History of Mary Prince – A West Indian Slave – Related by Herself* (first published in 1831) Pandora, London 1987

Fryer, Peter *Staying Power – The History of Black People in Britain* Pluto Press, London 1984

Hubbard, Vincent K Swords *Ships and Sugar – History of Nevis* Premiere Editions International, Corvallis, Oregon 2002

Inikori, Joseph E and Engerman, Stanley L (eds) *The Atlantic Slave Trade – Effects on Economies, Societies, and Peoples in Africa, the Americas, and Europe* Duke University Press, London 1992

Jones, Pip and Youseph, Rita *The Black Population of Bristol in the Eighteenth Century*, Bristol Branch of the Historical Association, Bristol 1994

Lambert, Sheila (ed) *House of Commons Sessional Papers of the Eighteenth Century* Scholarly Resources, Delaware, Irish University Press 1975

Lewis, Matthew Gregory *Journal of a Residence Among the Negroes in the West Indies* John Murray, London 1845

Litchfield, R B *Tom Wedgwood* Duckworth, London 1903

Minchinton, Walter E (ed) *The Trade of Bristol in the Eighteenth Century* Bristol Record Society, vol XX 1957

Muñoz, Sharon R *The Afro-American Griot Speaks: Afro American Names* James C Winston, Nashville, Tennessee 1995

Olwig, Karen Fog *Global Culture, Island Identity – Continuing Change in the Afro-Caribbean Community of Nevis* Harwood Academic Publishers, Chur, Switzerland 1993

Sheridan, Richard B *Sugar and Slavery: an Economic History of the British West Indies 1623-1775*, Caribbean Universities Press, Barbados 1974 and 1994

Sketchley's Bristol Directory 1775 Kingsmead Reprints, Bath 1971

Stewart , Julia *1001 African Names*, Carol Publishing 1997

Thomas, Hugh *The History of the Atlantic Slave Trade 1440-1870* Picador, London 1997

Tyson, George F and Highfield, Arnold R (eds) *The Kamina Folk – Slavery and Slave Life in the Danish West Indies* Virgin Islands Humanities Council, US Virgin Islands 1994

Walvin, James *Black Ivory* Fontana Press, London 1992